MARIA DOLORES BRANNAN
*was born in Dewsbury in Yorkshire.
She studied textile design at Dewsbury
& Batley Art College and Cumbria
Art College, leaving to pursue a career
in this field. Beginning by selling
hand-knits at trade fairs, she has gone
on to assist such celebrated designers as
Kaffe Fassett and Jill Gordon.*

    *For the past ten years, she has been
living and working as a textile designer
in London. This is her first book.*

TAPESTRY

W O R K S T A T I O N

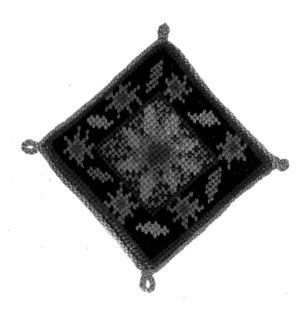

MARIA DOLORES BRANNAN

WORKSTATION *is a new concept comprising all the elements you will need to commence the fascinating art of tapestry. The first 48 pages of this book offer a full colour introduction to tapestry including a selection of beautiful and original projects which will guide the user through basic skills to more advanced techniques. The remaining 24 pages at the back of the book are printed with the charts required to create the projects. While basically structured as a beginners' course, the book contains many designs that will appeal to more experienced stitchers, including the Fruit Lampshade with its rainbow blend of yarns and the magnificent Houses Cushion featuring a patchwork of 12 individual house fronts.*

A DESIGN EYE BOOK
First published in 1996 by
Design Eye Limited
The Corn Exchange, Market Square,
Bishop's Stortford,
Herts CM23 3XF

ISBN 187270056X

Photography by Paul Forrester
Art direction by Tessa Dennison
Edited by Patsy North
Illustrations by John Hutchinson
Editorial and design on this book by
Craft Plus Publishing Ltd.

Dedication
To my Dad, Derick James Brannan

Acknowledgements
I would like to thank the following companies for supplying yarn and
canvas for the projects in this book:
Yarns: Paterna Yarns, The Craft Collection, PO Box 1,
Ossett, West Yorkshire WF5 9SA. Telephone: 01924 811905
Canvas: William Briggs, School Street,
Bromley Cross, Bolton BL7 9PA.
Telephone: 01204 302181

I would also like to thank David Forest and
Beverley Stratton for their help with
stitching the projects, Matthew McGuchan
for his valuable assistance and all my
family for always being supportive.

Printed in China

CONTENTS

INTRODUCTION

On the following pages I shall be introducing you to the craft of tapestry, otherwise known as needlepoint or canvaswork. This ancient technique of stitching coloured yarn into canvas has been used through the centuries to create designs that are both functional and decorative.

Tapestry Workstation has been structured with the first-time embroiderer in mind. There are eleven projects, organized to lead you from the simplest stitches and patterns to more advanced stitches and elaborate designs. All the projects are accompanied by charts, located in the back of the book on pages that can be pulled out for convenience. The use of the charts is explained in the chapter called 'Setting To Work' on page 20.

The kit that accompanies **Tapestry Workstation** contains all the materials you will need to make the 'Rose' tapestry from Project One. Information to help you when purchasing further yarns and canvas can be found in the chapter entitled Materials & Equipment. Also included in the book are a Stitch Dictionary that illustrates all the stitches used in the projects, and a section describing my personal sources of inspiration.

I've always loved colour and pattern, and find great satisfaction in using my hands creatively. Tapestry combines all these elements and has given me many hours of pleasure over the years. What could be better than to enjoy the motion of stitching and then to have a beautiful end result to decorate your home or to give as a present?

In this age of mass-produced goods, the ability to create decorative and functional hand-made objects becomes increasingly precious. Modern stitchers can draw not only upon the knowledge left to us by past generations but also upon a wide spectrum of yarn colours, giving us great opportunities to produce our own imaginative new compositions.

I hope that this book will not only teach you the skills of tapestry which, as you will discover as you try some of the projects, are actually quite simple, but will also inspire you to go on and design your own personal pieces of work.

$\mathcal{M}$ATERIALS &
$\mathcal{E}$QUIPMENT

$\mathcal{T}$he materials and equipment you will need to begin stitching a piece of tapestry are very simple: a length of canvas, some yarn, a tapestry needle and a pair of scissors.

$\mathcal{B}$efore you purchase any materials it is important that you read through the following pages, which will give you a better understanding of the qualities and benefits of the many different types available on the market.

$\mathcal{C}$ANVAS

When buying canvas it is essential to make a careful choice, as the canvas is the foundation of any tapestry design. Make sure that the canvas you choose is of good quality, with no knots or breaks in the thread.

Consider the design you are about to stitch. If the design is predominantly made up of pale colours, then you should opt for white canvas. This is because a small amount of the canvas will inevitably show through between certain types of stitch. Do bear in mind, however, that white canvas can be hard on the eyes, particularly in the finer gauges. A darker design should be stitched onto fawn-coloured canvas, known as 'antique'.

Canvas is often made of cotton or linen, although any material with a regular grid structure can be used, including plastic. There are several types of canvas: the most common types used are plain single-thread, interlock single and double-thread.

From left to right: interlock, double, single-thread and plastic canvas.

Single-thread or **mono canvas** consists of a grid of horizontal and vertical threads woven over and under each other. Because the canvas threads are not locked together at the cross-over points, it means that this canvas is not suitable for use with certain stitches. Half-cross stitch, for instance, only crosses one thread at the back of the work and so will slip under the warp and unravel if pulled tight. You must make sure that designs stitched on this canvas are worked in tent stitch, which goes over two threads at the back and will not unravel.

Single-thread canvas is available in a wide range of gauges as shown above.

The advantage of mono canvas is its flexibility – because it has a lot of 'give', it is ideal for items such as cushion covers. Mono canvas is not suitable to use for projects set within a rigid frame – a drop-in chair seat, for example– because it will soon stretch out of shape.

Interlock canvas also has a single-mesh structure but is bound at the cross-over points. All tapestry stitches can be worked on this canvas. It also has the advantage of not unravelling when cut, making it ideal for small or shaped items. Stitched interlock canvas forms a very sturdy fabric ideal to use for upholstered seats.

This picture shows the size of stitch achieved with different gauge canvases.

Where the type of canvas is not specified in the You Will Need list with each project, any canvas is suitable. If it is important to use a particular type, this will be listed.

Double-thread canvas, also known as Penelope, has a double mesh construction, formed by the intersection of pairs of vertical threads with pairs of horizontal threads. With double-thread canvas you can form stitches of different sizes within the same design – when the pairs of threads are separated, four plain meshes are formed that are capable of receiving smaller stitches. You can also insert the needle between paired horizontal canvas threads when using straight stitches to give a smoother line to a curve. We will be taking advantage of these features in the Twelve Houses Cushion on page 46. Double-thread is the strongest of the different canvas types, ideal for chair-seats and upholstery that will receive heavy wear.

Plastic canvas, as its name implies, is made of plastic and has a single-mesh structure. It is ideal for items which need to be rigid, such as boxes, or for small, complex shapes such as brooches or Christmas tree ornaments as the canvas can be cut close to the stitching without fraying.

Canvas gauges All of the canvas types can be bought in a range of gauges. The gauge of a canvas is the number of threads contained per 2.5cm (1in). Thus 10-gauge canvas has 10 threads per 2.5cm (1in). In the case of double-thread canvas the gauge number refers to the number of pairs of threads – 10-gauge double-thread canvas has 10 pairs of threads (twenty individual strands) per 2.5cm (1in). Note that when the instructions given in this book refer to a 'thread', in the case of double-thread canvas this refers to a pair of threads.
As long as you make sure that the canvas you buy to stitch a particular design has the correct gauge as stated in the instructions, you are free to choose whichever type of canvas you feel is most suitable for the final use of your finished tapestry.

The samples on the left show the effects that can be achieved when stitching on double-thread canvas. With double thread canvas, you can produce finer versions of stitches by working into the holes between the pairs of threads.

YARNS

Tapestry can be worked using a number of different types of thread. All that is essential is that the thread is thin enough to slide easily through the holes of the canvas but thick enough to cover the canvas in stitch form. In general, the larger the canvas mesh (i.e. the fewer holes there are per 2.5cm (1in) and the lower the gauge number), the thicker the thread you should use. The yarns most commonly used for tapestry designs are Persian yarn, tapestry wool and crewel wool.

Persian yarn is the yarn that I have chosen to use for the projects in this book. Because it is made of three intertwined threads, Persian yarn is very versatile. You can easily separate the individual threads, using them singly or doubled depending on the gauge of the canvas. You can also mix different coloured yarns together to give a smooth blend when changing from one colour to the next.

Tapestry wool is relatively thick and is used as a single strand. Unlike Persian yarn, it cannot be split into separate threads. It is suitable for medium-gauge canvas, particularly 12-gauge.

Crewel wool is a very fine wool which can be used as a single strand for detailed work on fine canvas or with several strands combined for slightly larger gauges of canvas.

As you become more confident in the art of tapestry, you may wish to experiment with other threads. In addition to those mentioned above, any reasonably strong thread of your choosing can be used, including embroidery threads, ribbons, silks and metallic threads. Knitting yarns are also suitable, but be sure to select those which are strong, smooth and not too elastic. With elastic yarns, there tends to be a problem maintaining tension across a tapestry.

Whichever yarns you choose to use for your tapestry work, it is worth working a small sample first, in the appropriate stitch, to check that they will cover the canvas adequately.

There is a tempting array of yarns in a vast spectrum of colours available to the embroiderer. You do not need not feel restricted to wool yarns; silk and cotton threads, metallic threads and even narrow ribbon can be used successfully in tapestry designs and can add an element of originality to your work.

From left to right below: metallic threads, a narrow silk ribbon, 6-stranded embroidery cotton and a wider silk ribbon.

Persian yarn

Tapestry wool

Crewel wool

NEEDLES

Tapestry needles are blunt-ended and have long eyes to accommodate the thicker yarns used. Sharp needles should not be used as they can damage the canvas threads.

Tapestry needles are available in a range of sizes. The higher the size-number, the finer the needle. The ideal size of needle is determined by the gauge of the canvas – the needle should be able to pass smoothly between the canvas threads without forcing them apart. The size of the needle eye should also be considered: too fine and the eye will fray the yarn, too large and the thread will slip around.

FRAMES

It is your choice whether or not to use a frame to support your canvas. Frames are not essential but do have some advantages, because they keep the canvas taut and prevent distortion of the design. They can be bought in a variety of sizes and styles, ranging from simple hand-held versions to elaborate floor-standing devices that will hold your work at a comfortable height and angle.

The main disadvantage of using a frame is that it will slow down the stitching process by not allowing you to make a single stitch in one movement. When the canvas is pulled tightly over the frame, two movements are required – pushing the yarn through to the back of the canvas, then again through to the front.

1 *Backstitch a length of webbing 2.5cm (1in) wide to the side edges of the canvas. Make a 1cm (⅜in) turning on the top and bottom edges and backstitch to the tapes on the rods of the frame, using strong sewing thread.*

2 *Assemble the frame, stretching the canvas taut. The method will vary depending on the type of frame. Lace the webbing to the frame at the sides with strong thread.*

OTHER TOOLS

❖ It is best to have two pairs of scissors: a large pair for cutting the canvas and a smaller, pointed pair for cutting the yarn and unpicking stitches if required.

❖ To transfer your design onto the canvas you must use a waterproof pen, because you will be damping your tapestry before stretching it, and a non-waterproof ink will run and discolour your work.

❖ For stretching, or blocking, your finished tapestry (see page 23), you need a piece of paper from which to cut a template, a white cloth to protect your tapestry, a sponge to dampen the work, rustproof nails or tacks and a hammer, a large flat board, a set-square and a ruler, and some wallpaper paste.

❖ It is also important to have a bright source of light, particularly when working on a fine-gauge canvas. Normal light-bulbs actually cast a yellowish light, which makes it hard to distinguish closely related hues; you may prefer to use a daylight bulb, which you can purchase from photographic or craft suppliers. This offers the same colour of light as normal daylight and makes it easier to achieve fine judgement of colour.

❖ Everyday sewing equipment, such as a tape measure, glass-headed pins and sewing thread, are necessary for making up the projects into finished items. If there are particular requirements, these will be explained within the project instructions.

Craft and embroidery scissors.

Waterproof pen.

Sewing thread.

Plasticized tape measure.

Glass headed pins.

Set square and rustproof tacks.

Needle case.

Sources of Inspiration

*A*ll you need to create your own tapestry design is an image that
inspires you and the confidence to make it your own. We have a
wealth of visual source material all around us to draw inspiration from.
Try taking ideas directly from nature, as I have done in
the Floral Cushion on page 28 or the Fruit
Lampshade on page 44, or use images from the
pages of books or magazines.

    The breadth of colour and form found in fine
art can also trigger off new ideas, and these can
often be successfully developed and translated
into tapestry designs. Textiles, painted ceramics,
architecture – all can provide the spark that
will set a new design in motion. The Lakai
Cushion and Tie-back on page 38 were based
on ethnic textile patterns, while the Twelve
Houses Cushion on page 46 was inspired by
decorative house fronts that appealed to me.

    It is a good idea to cut out and keep pictures
that inspire you in a folder, so that you will have
a constant source of reference to work from.

Stitch Dictionary

The tapestry stitches used in the projects in the book are listed alphabetically on the following six pages. You may need to vary the number of canvas threads over which they are worked, depending on the project. Check with the instructions and the chart you are working from to see if this is the case.

Algerian Eye Stitch

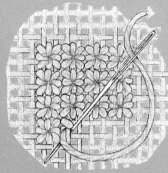

Form eight stitches into a square unit, each crossing one thread of canvas and sharing a central hole. The square can be enlarged by working each stitch over more than one thread. Adjoining squares share the same canvas holes.

Algerian Filling Stitch

This quick filling stitch can be worked vertically or horizontally across the canvas. It consists of groups of three straight stitches, each worked over four canvas threads. Each group of stitches is placed four threads away from the previous one. The second row is worked in the opposite direction, stepping the groups of stitches so they fit two threads up between the gaps as shown.

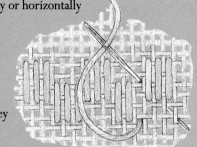

Basketweave Stitch

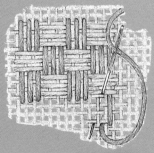

Work groups of three horizontal and vertical stitches, covering four canvas threads. In the next row, the vertical stitches are below the horizontal stitches from the previous row and vice versa. Use two contrasting colours, one for the horizontal and another for the vertical stitches to create a check pattern.

Brick Stitch

Each stitch covers two canvas threads and is worked in single rows of stitches forming a zigzag pattern across the canvas. Work the first row from right to left and the second row from left to right, fitting the stitches into the zigzag shape produced by the first row and re-using the holes previously used.

Byzantine Stitch

This stitch is worked diagonally across the canvas in a stepped pattern, alternating narrow and wider rows. Work over as many canvas thread intersections as is shown on the chart you are working from and in the direction shown. Follow the chart outlines for the step pattern which is usually stitched in two colours for a bold striped effect.

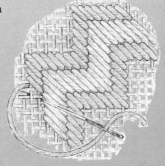

Cross Stitch

This stitch is formed by making two diagonal stitches which cross each other. Work over as many canvas thread intersections as required to obtain the right-sized cross. To achieve a neat appearance, ensure that the top 'legs' of the stitches always cross in the same direction.

Cushion Stitch

Cushion stitch consists of simple square units made up of diagonal stitches worked in opposite directions along each row. A single unit comprises five stitches worked diagonally over one, two three, two and one intersections of canvas threads. Each square in the pattern shares the same holes as the ones on each side of it, with the stitches sloping in opposite directions, giving an interesting geometric effect across the canvas.

Diamond Eyelet Stitch

Each diamond consists of 16 stitches sharing a central hole. The adjoining diamond units share the same canvas holes. Add backstitches, each covering one canvas thread intersection, to hide the exposed canvas threads between the diamond units.

Double Cross Stitch

Make a large cross stitch over the required number of canvas threads. Work a vertical cross stitch over the top of it, ending with a horizontal stitch. As with cross stitch, a neater effect will be achieved if all the individual stages of the stitch are worked in the same direction.

French Knot

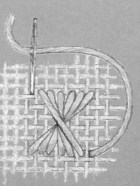

Bring the needle out one hole below where you want the stitch to be. Holding the thread taut with one hand, wrap the thread around the needle once and insert the needle back into the canvas one thread above the original.

You can vary the size of knot produced by winding the yarn around the needle more than once. Try a few on some spare canvas until you achieve the required effect.

Half Rhodes Stitch

This is a simpler version of Rhodes stitch (see page 18). First make a diagonal stitch sloping from bottom left to top right to set the size of the square design you require. Using the holes one to the right at the bottom and one to the left at the top, work a sequence of stitches until the final diagonal stitch is in place. This stitch can be worked either vertically or horizontally on your canvas. A small bar can be worked at the cross-over point for extra decoration.

Hungarian Stitch

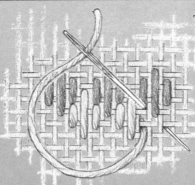

This stitch can be worked vertically or horizontally. One stitch over four canvas threads is flanked by two smaller stitches over two canvas threads. The second row interlocks with the first.

Jacquard Stitch

The stitches are worked diagonally in stepped rows. Follow the outlined step design on the appropriate chart and work in the direction shown in the diagram on the right.

This stitch can be worked in a single colour, or for a dramatic, geometric effect, use a darker colour for the smaller, outer stitches.

Leaf Stitch

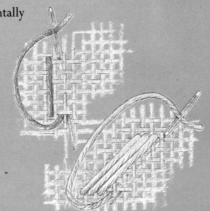

Each leaf consists of 11 stitches, three at each side and five fanned out at the top. Adjoining leaves share canvas holes at the sides. Start each successive row six holes down and place the leaves so that they interlock with the leaves above.

Long Satin Stitch

This stitch can be worked either vertically, horizontally or diagonally over as many canvas threads as required. It consists of long straight stitches worked alongside one another and is useful for filling narrow areas of canvas.

Try to ensure that the stitches are not worked over so many threads that long, loopy strands are produced. These could become snagged when the finished tapestry is in use, giving the work an unprofessional finish.

Mosaic Stitch

This is worked in square units, each with three diagonal stitches. The longer stitch covers two canvas threads, the two smaller stitches just one canvas thread.

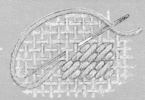

Random Long Stitch

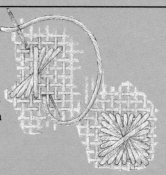

This is worked in varying lengths of straight stitches either horizontally or vertically over the canvas, each stitch covering a different number of canvas threads. The interlocking stitches share the same canvas holes.

Rhodes Stitch

Work this as for Half Rhodes Stitch (see page 16), but continue the stitches around the square design to complete the shape. The size can be varied and can be finished with a small, straight bar stitch across the middle. This will hold the longer loops in place, preventing them from becoming caught when the finished piece of work is in use.

Rya Stitch

This stitch is worked as rows of loops that can be cut if desired. Insert the needle from the front of the canvas and make a horizontal backstitch over two canvas threads (a). Form a loop and make another backstitch (b). Continue in this way along the row (c). Work the stitches in the next row so that the loops hang over the top of the stitches in the previous row (d).

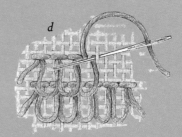

a

b

c

d

Scottish Stitch

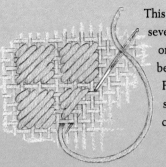

This square stitch consists of seven diagonal stitches. Leave one thread of canvas between the square units. Fill the gaps between the squares with tent stitch in a contrasting colour.

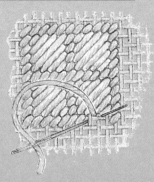

Tent Stitch

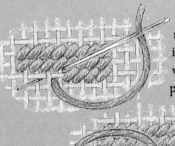

This is the most commonly used needlepoint stitch. It produces a strong, hard-wearing finish and is quick and easy to work. Always work this stitch with the canvas stretched on a slate frame to prevent it from becoming too distorted.

Each stitch is worked diagonally from bottom left to top right. Work the first row from right to left. Turn the canvas around to work the second row, again from right to left. Or, work back across the canvas from left to right as shown.

Velvet Stitch

Make a diagonal and a vertical stitch, holding a small loop of thread with the thumb (a). Make a diagonal stitch, forming a cross (b). Continue from left to right to form a row of loops (c and d).

a

b

c

d

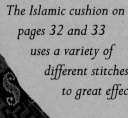

The Islamic cushion on pages 32 and 33 uses a variety of different stitches to great effect.

SETTING TO WORK

Before you begin stitching a project, you will need to know how to cut out and prepare your canvas, and also how to follow the chart given with the design. Once your project is complete, the tapestry will need to be stretched before being made up. It is important to follow the advice in this chapter carefully so that you can be sure of achieving a professional–looking finish with every item you make.

PREPARING THE CANVAS

Your piece of canvas should be cut to allow a border of at least 5cm (2in) all around the design. Make sure that the line of your scissors follows the line of the canvas thread (fig 1), otherwise the canvas will unravel. Even with a shaped design

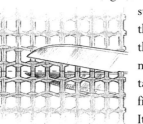

such as the Curtain Tie-Back on page 38, follow the line of the canvas thread, forming a rectangle big enough to allow the 5cm (2in) minimum border (fig 2). This will make it much easier to stretch your canvas back into shape when the tapestry is finished.

▼ *fig 2*

It is a good idea to seal

▲ *fig 1*

the edge of the canvas either with a hem or with some masking tape to stop the yarn you are using (or your sleeves) from catching on any rough edges.

FROM CHART TO CANVAS

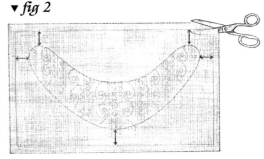

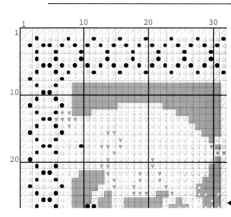

If you look through the design charts at the back of the book, you will see that there are two types — those that use symbols and those that use outlines.

Simple designs The smaller designs are plotted stitch-by-stitch onto graph paper, with different symbols used to represent the different colours (figs 3 and 4). Any unusual stitches have been illustrated on the chart or

◄ *fig 3* described separately.

Each square of the chart represents a single
intersection of a horizontal and a vertical canvas thread,
NOT a hole. The number of rows or columns of the chart
that you count corresponds to the number of threads.
This may seem a little confusing at first, but you will soon
get used to it.

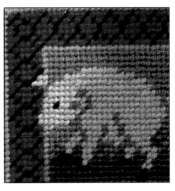

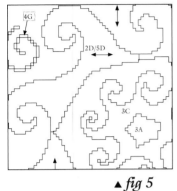

▲ fig 4   **▼ fig 6**

Advanced designs For the
larger or more advanced
designs that come later in the
book, outline charts have
been provided. In these charts
the areas of different stitch
types and different colours
have been denoted by letters
and numerals with a key
(figs 5 and 6).

▲ fig 5

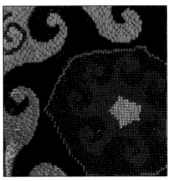

Enlarging your Chart

All the outline charts have been reduced in size to fit on the pages at the back of
this book and will need to be enlarged to their actual sizes using a photocopier.
In each case, instructions have been provided with the chart giving the
percentage increase you need in order to photocopy it up to size. In some cases,
this will take several stages and you should expect to end up with a number of
separate sheets. Ask your stationer for assistance if you are uncertain about how
to do this. You can now stick your separate sheets together to reveal the actual
design size. The resulting shape can also be used as your template when
stretching the finished needlepoint.

Transferring the design You can now transfer the
design onto the canvas using a *waterproof* marker pen by
simply placing the canvas over the scaled-up photocopy
and tracing the design through (fig 7).
**YOU MUST MAKE SURE THAT THE HORIZONTAL AND
VERTICAL LINES OF THE CHART CORRESPOND EXACTLY
TO THE HORIZONTAL AND VERTICAL THREADS ON THE
CANVAS.** The importance of this will become clear as
you begin stitching.

▲ fig 7

You do not need to draw in the exact 'stepped' outlines of the motifs;
it is sufficient to draw smooth outlines. These smooth outlines are to be used as a
guide and will become stepped as you place your stitches. Refer back to the
chart for more detailed information.

*A final tip – it is a good idea to draw an arrow on your canvas to indicate
which way up the design is. It is very easy to come back from a break and begin
placing your stitches in the wrong direction, so take care!*

STARTING TO STITCH

If you are intending to use a frame you can now attach your canvas to it. For stitching, use lengths of yarn that are no longer than 50cm (20in). A longer length of yarn than this will prove difficult to work with, not only because it is likely to become tangled, but also because with repeated passes through the canvas the yarn will become increasingly worn. Weak, thin yarn will not cover the canvas properly.

Be careful not to make your stitches too tight, as this will also affect canvas coverage, and will make the finished piece extremely difficult to stretch back into the correct shape.

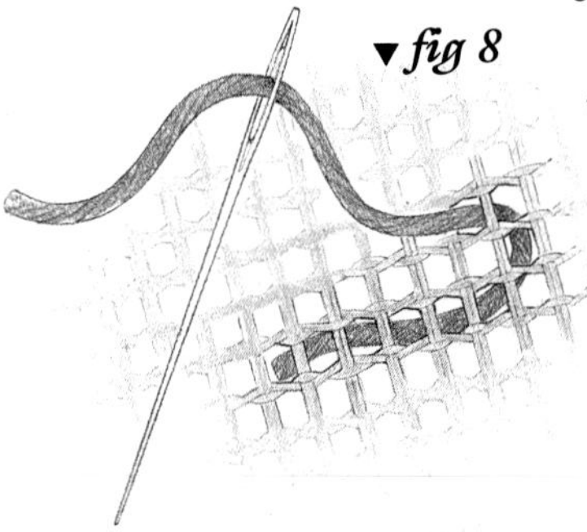

▼ *fig 8* When you make your first stitch, start by pushing the needle through from the back of the canvas to the front, leaving a tail of at least 2.5cm (1in) of thread protruding out of the back of the work (fig 8). You can secure this tail by holding it flat against the canvas and catching it in the loop of your next stitch (fig 9). You can repeat this several times with subsequent stitches to make sure the tail of thread is firmly held (fig 10). When you have finished with a particular thread, make sure you darn a length of at least 2.5cm ▲ *fig 9* (1in) neatly through the stitches on the back of the canvas before cutting the thread (fig 11). If you are now going to start a new colour you can either repeat the process described above, or if your new colour is going to sit adjacent to an area that has already been stitched, you can secure the new yarn by threading it through existing stitches on the back of the canvas.

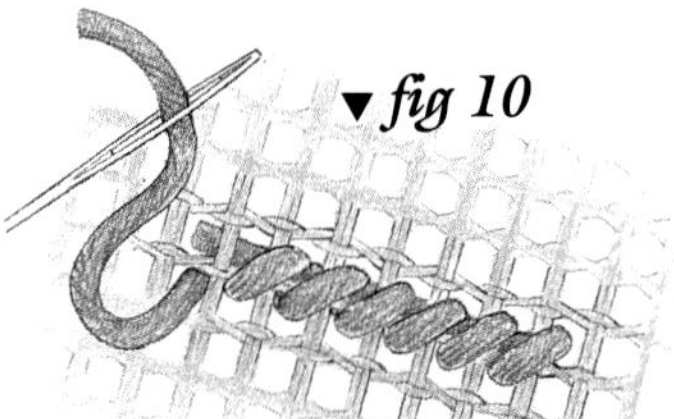

▼ *fig 10*

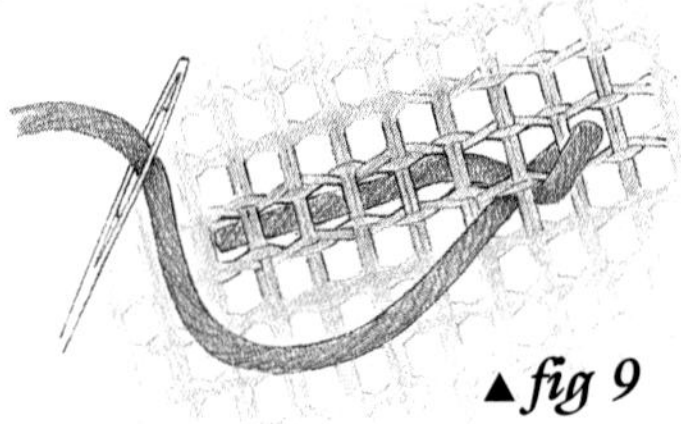

▼ *fig 11*

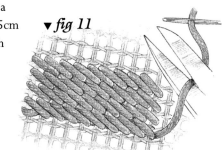

If you wish to continue using the same thread in a different area, draw that thread through existing stitches on the back of the canvas to reach your new starting-point, as long as this is not too far away. Avoid leaving loops of yarn on the back of your canvas.

STITCHING TIPS

❖ *When working from a symbol chart, I always find it useful to stitch in the outline edges of the design before beginning the body of the stitching, simply to make sure that I have placed the design in the centre of the canvas. If you wish to work in this way, begin stitching 5cm (2in) in from each edge at one of the corners. It is essential to double-check that the number of stitches in your outline is correct. If there are any other obvious structural lines – for instance, inner border lines around a central image – it is also a good idea to stitch these in now.*

❖ *It is sometimes recommended that you start from the centre of the design and work outwards, or that you stitch the light colours first, then the darks, and then the colours in-between. I would say that it is up to you to work in the way that suits you best.*

STRETCHING AND BLOCKING

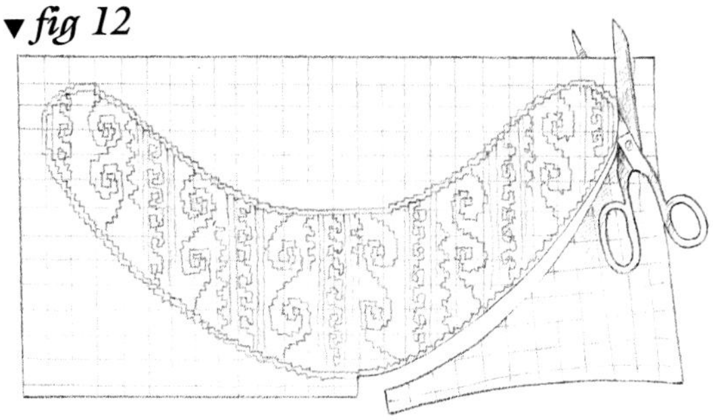

The process of stitching inevitably pulls the design out of its intended shape. When you have finished stitching, it is necessary to stretch your work back into shape. This process is known as blocking.

▼ *fig 12*

The first step is to make a paper template that is the same shape and size as your design, using your original measurements. If you have photocopied the chart up to scale, you can simply cut around the outline of the design to form the template (fig 12).

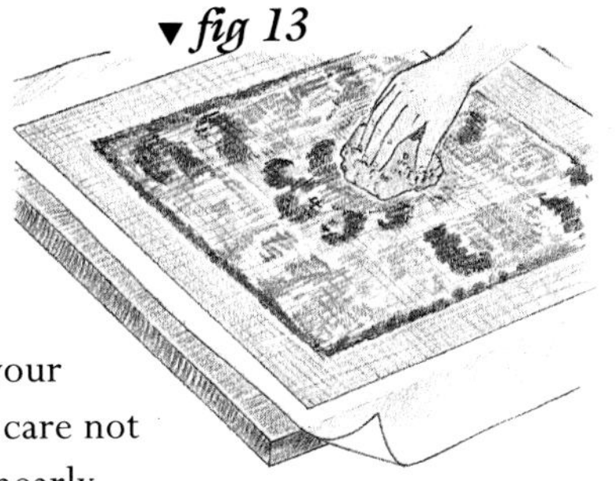

You will now need a piece of board big enough to give you a margin of at least 10cm (4in) around your canvas, and thick enough to take the length of the rustproof nails or tacks that you are going to use. Lay a piece of white cloth over the board and place your tapestry face down. Dampen the back of your canvas using a sponge and warm water (fig 13). Take care not to use excessive water – although tapestry yarns are nearly always colourfast, it is better to err on the side of caution.

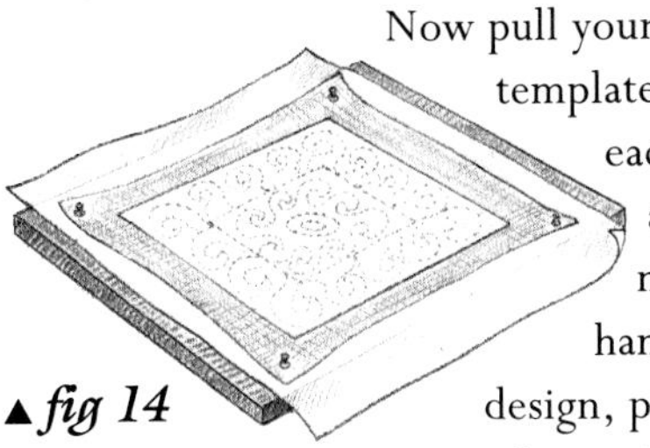

▼ *fig 13*

Now pull your canvas into the correct shape, using the template to guide you. Hammer a nail or tack through each corner of your canvas into the board, leaving a distance of at least 2.5cm (1in) between the nail and the stitched area (fig 14). Keep hammering nails in around the edges of the design, pulling the canvas tight as you go, until it has resumed its original proportions. The nails will probably need to be spaced at intervals of 6mm–12mm (¼in–½in) by the time you have finished (fig 15). You can check that the corners of your design are at the correct angle by using a set-square.

▲ *fig 14*

When you have finished nailing, use a brush to cover the back of the canvas with a thin layer of wallpaper paste. As the paste dries, it will hold the stitches firmly in place and prevent further distortion of the work.

Leave the board in a warm place and let the tapestry dry completely before attempting to remove it from the board. This will take at least 48 hours.

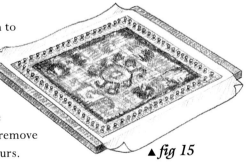

▲ *fig 15*

MAKING UP

However you choose to make up your finished project, remember **YOU MUST NOT CUT THE CANVAS TOO CLOSE TO THE EDGE OF THE TAPESTRY**, as some canvas types will fray easily. Depending on the item you are making, simply leave 1.3cm-2.5cm (½in-1in) of canvas around the design to use as a seam allowance or fold under as required.

SIMPLE FLOWER SQUARES

For this first project we shall be working solely in tent stitch, the most common needlepoint stitch (see Stitch Dictionary, page 19). I also want to introduce you to the use of simple design elements known as 'motifs', and to the use of the border. A motif is a small shape that can be repeated within a design to give it a sense of pattern and theme. Traditional motifs include flower and leaf shapes. A repeated motif is often used to form a border. Simple but attractive designs can be created by taking an image and enclosing it with a border containing the image in motif form.

~You Will Need~

For each square measuring
10cm x 10cm (4in x 4in):

❖ 20cm x 20cm (8in x 8in)
  10-gauge canvas
❖ Stranded Persian yarn, one skein in each of the colours as given with the charts on page II
❖ Tapestry needle

STITCHING

Having read through Setting to Work (see page 20), you are ready to begin

The yarns and canvas for the Rose Square have been supplied in your Tapestry Workstation kit, along with a needle. A piece of backing fabric has also been included; you can use this to make up the project as a pincushion, a purse or a pot pourri sachet instead of a framed picture.

stitching. Use **two strands only** of Persian yarn throughout. Following the charts on page II, work the Flower Squares in tent stitch. Block the tapestries (see page 23).

MAKING UP

❖ **Rose Square** Mount and frame professionally.
❖ **Daisy Square** Backstitch a square of fabric to the tapestry with right sides facing. Turn through and add zip, lining and cord to make a purse.
❖ **Primula Square** Backstitch a fabric square around three sides with right sides facing. Turn through, stuff and sew last side to make a pincushion.

These three flower squares are simple to work if you have never tried tapestry before. They are, from the top, the Primula Square, Daisy Square and Rose Square.

FARMYARD PANEL

*P*roject Two is another set of variations on the simple square. Each of these light–hearted farmyard designs has a geometric border that provides a surround to the central animal. I have mounted the three designs in one frame, but you could choose your favourite design and mount it up separately. Each square measures 10cm x 10cm (4in x 4in).

   Once again I have restricted myself to tent stitch for these designs. They are quick and easy to work by counting the squares on the charts provided.

~You Will Need~

For a panel measuring 40cm x 16cm (5½in x 15¾in):

❖ Three 20cm (8in) squares 10-gauge canvas
❖ Stranded Persian yarn in the colours as given with the charts on page III
❖ Tapestry needle

STITCHING THE DESIGN

Use **two strands only** of Persian yarn throughout. Following the charts on page III, work the Farmyard designs in tent stitch.

FINISHING OFF

Block the finished squares of tapestry (see page 23). For

the best result for your panel, it is advisable to have the three animal squares mounted and framed professionally.

   Alternatively, you can make your own mount from plain acid-free board. Cut three equally spaced apertures of the correct size for the tapestry pictures, using a scalpel or craft knife and a metal ruler. Then secure the pictures behind the apertures with double-sided tape. You can now frame the panel as you wish.

Each of these farmyard animals has a different colourful border. The animals overlap the frames in places, giving the pictures a three–dimensional effect.

27

Floral Cushion

A strong, simple floral motif is used as the basis of this bright cushion design in tent stitch. Each of the main flowers has a single colour at its centre and two colours for the petals. Dispersed among these are smaller blue flowers and green leaves.

~You Will Need~

For a cushion measuring 41cm x 41cm
(16in x 16in):

- 51cm x 51cm (20in x 20in)
  7-gauge canvas
- Stranded Persian yarn in the
  colours as given with the
  chart on pages IV–V
- 45cm x 55cm (17.5in x 21.5in)
  backing fabric
- 1.8m (2yd) piping cord
- 1.8m (2yd) blue bias binding
- Tapestry needle
- Cushion pad to fit

This striking cushion is worked entirely in tent stitch on 7-gauge canvas, making it a perfect project for a beginner who would like to stitch something a little bit more challenging.

Stitching

Use **three strands** of Persian yarn throughout. Following the chart on pages IV–V, work the Floral Cushion in tent stitch only throughout.

The best way to start is to stitch an outline of 112 stitches by 112 stitches in the background colour. Position this outline in the centre of the piece of canvas, leaving a 5cm (2in) border of unworked canvas all round.

ℳAKING UP

When the design is complete, block the canvas (see page 23). Trim the excess canvas from around the design to leave a 1.5cm seam allowance. Cut the backing fabric in half widthways and hem one long edge on each piece.

Cover the piping cord with the bias binding and with all the raw edges matching, tack in place around the outer edges of the cushion. With right sides facing, pin the backing fabric in place over the cushion front, overlapping the hemmed edges at centre back.

Stitch all round the edges, with backstitch or a straight machine stitch, making sure that the bias binding is caught in the seam.

Clip across the corners to remove the excess fabric and then turn the cushion cover through to the right side. Insert the cushion pad.

FISH PICTURE

This picture introduces two new stitches. The main part of the design is worked in tent stitch, as before, but for the fins and tail of the fish I have used satin stitch. As you can see in the photograph, these long, directional stitches are ideal for representing the shape and form of fins. The French knots I have used to put bubbles into the water are graduated in size by winding the yarn around the needle in one or more twists. See the Stitch Dictionary, starting on page 14, for details of how to work satin stitch and French knots.

~You Will Need~

For a picture measuring 18cm x 23cm (7in x 9in):

- 28cm x 33cm (11in x 13in) 7-gauge canvas
- Stranded Persian yarn in the colours as given with the chart on pages VI–VII
- Tapestry needle

STITCHING

Use **all three strands** of Persian yarn throughout. Following the chart on pages VI–VII, work the Fish Picture mainly in tent stitch, adding satin stitch and French knots where indicated on the chart.

The best way to start the picture is to stitch an outer border of 62 stitches wide and 48 stitches deep in the background colour. Position this outline in the centre of your piece of canvas, leaving a 5cm (2in)

The jolly fish in the picture above is worked mainly in tent stitch with satin stitch for the fins and French knots for the bubbles.

border of unworked canvas all the way around it.

The satin stitch areas are outlined on the chart. Work the two large fins in orange, gold and yellow, slanting the stitches to follow the outlines and create a realistic effect. For the smaller fins, use gold and yellow only, but slanting the stitches as before. Use the picture as a guide.

The bubbles are worked as graduated French knots. For the larger ones near the fish's mouth, wind the yarn around the needle several times before taking it back through to the right side. Decrease the number of times the yarn is wound around the needle as you progress up the picture – the small knots may only require one twist.

MAKING UP

When the design is complete, block the canvas to restore it to a square shape, taking care not to flatten any of the raised stitches (see page 23 for more details of how to do this).

You can have the picture mounted and framed by a professional framer. Alternatively, you can cut a mount yourself to fit an existing frame. For the best results, use a sharp craft knife and a metal ruler and cut the mount slightly smaller than the finished picture size to ensure that none of the unworked canvas around the edges will show.

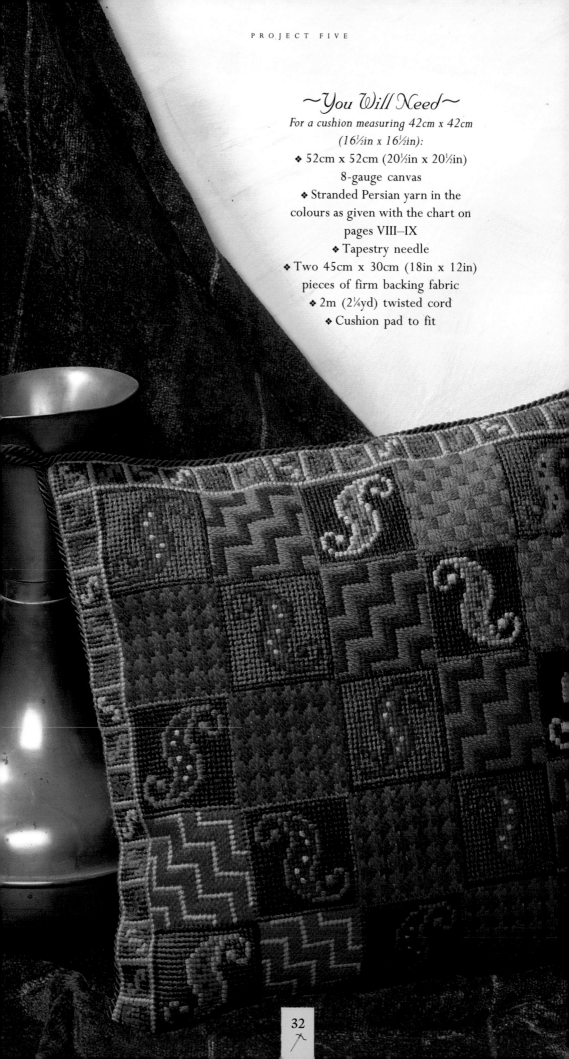

~*You Will Need*~

For a cushion measuring 42cm x 42cm
(16½in x 16½in):

❖ 52cm x 52cm (20½in x 20½in)
8-gauge canvas
❖ Stranded Persian yarn in the
colours as given with the chart on
pages VIII–IX
❖ Tapestry needle
❖ Two 45cm x 30cm (18in x 12in)
pieces of firm backing fabric
❖ 2m (2¼yd) twisted cord
❖ Cushion pad to fit

ISLAMIC CUSHION

This patchwork cushion is made up of simple geometric patterns and a motif inspired by traditional Islamic design. The motif is worked in tent stitch, but the border is a combination of tent stitch and cross stitch, and the other squares of the design are covered by a variety of different stitches. I have charted the areas of tent stitch using symbols as for the previous projects, but I have used outlines to define the areas where different stitches are used. These stitches are illustrated in the Stitch Dictionary on page 14.

STITCHING

Use **all three strands** of Persian yarn throughout. Following the chart on pages VIII–!X, first stitch the main yellow border outlines and the outlines of the inner squares in tent stitch. Work the small 'S'-shapes and dots around the border in cross stitch over one canvas intersection, then fill in the background in tent stitch. Similarly, work the outlines of the large 'S'-shapes and the single dots on the patchwork squares in cross stitch; fill in the background in tent stitch. Work the other patchwork squares in the stitches shown in the key.

MAKING UP

Block the tapestry (see page 23). Trim the canvas to 1.5cm (⅝in) all round. Hem one long side of each piece of backing fabric. Pin the fabric pieces to the tapestry with right sides together and the hemmed edges overlapping at centre back. Stitch all round with backstitch or by machine, taking a 1.5cm (⅝in) seam allowance. Clip the corners, turn through and insert the cushion pad. Trim with twisted cord.

Noël, Noël

These festive designs gave me a wonderful excuse to use all the brightest yarn colours I could find, together with a gold yarn, to produce eye-catching tree decorations and a stocking.

~You Will Need~

- ❖ 40cm x 30cm (16in x 12in) 8-gauge canvas
- ❖ 40cm x 30cm (16in x 12in) backing fabric
- ❖ 12cm (5in) red twisted cord
- ❖ 15cm x 11cm (6in x 4½in) 8-gauge plastic canvas (for each decoration)
- ❖ Stranded Persian yarn in the colours as given with the chart on pages X–XI
- ❖ 1 ball of metallic gold 4-ply knitting yarn
- ❖ Tapestry needle

STOCKING

Use **two strands** of yarn except for the long diagonal stitches, which need **all three**. Enlarge the chart on page XI to 165% and trace squarely onto the canvas. Work the design using the stitches shown. When the design is complete, trim the canvas, leaving 1.5cm (⅝in) all round. With right sides facing, sew on a fabric backing. Clip the seams and turn through. Turn under the raw edge at the top. Attach a cord for hanging.

TREE JOYS

Use **three strands** of yarn and cross stitch onto plastic canvas, using the charts on page X. Trim to one canvas thread, neaten edges and attach a hanging loop.

DAISY FRAME

For this attractive and functional picture or mirror frame, the daisy motif from Project One is alternated with geometric squares that include a number of new stitches. The chart for the design is a combination of symbols and outlines, so count your stitches carefully when following it. I have used interlock canvas for the project – when making up the frame, you have to cut right up to the inner corners of your tapestry, so you need a canvas that will not fray.

~You Will Need~

For a frame measuring 33cm x 26cm
(13in x 10¼in):

❖ 43cm x 38cm (17in x 15in)
12-gauge interlock canvas
❖ Stranded Persian yarn as given with the
chart on pages XII–XIII
❖ Tapestry needle
❖ Two pieces of stiff card
33cm x 26cm (13in x 10¼in)
❖ 36cm x 29cm backing fabric

STITCHING

Use **two strands only** of Persian yarn
throughout. Follow the chart and
instructions on pages XII–XIII.

This stunning picture frame has a chequered
border made up of bright daisy motifs and
panels of different needlepoint stitches. See
the Stitch Dictionary on pages 14 to 19 for
full details of how to work the appropriate
areas of the design.

Making up the Frame

Block the tapestry (see page 23). Cut around the outer and
inner edges of the design, leaving 2.5cm (1in) of unworked
canvas all round. Clip diagonally into the inner
corners. Cut a centre hole out of one of the pieces
of card. Place your tapestry over it and fold the
inner canvas edges around the hole. Secure at the
back with masking tape.

Place the picture behind the aperture. Lay the
other piece of card on the back and fold the outer
edge of the tapestry around it. Secure with tape.
Fold under 1.5cm (⅝in) all round the piece of
backing fabric and slip stitch to the frame back.

LAKAI CUSHION & TIE-BACK

This project was inspired by the traditional embroideries of the Lakai tribe of Northern Afghanistan, who have been producing distinctive designs for over 100 years, characterized by sharp-edged patterns and areas of flat, saturated colour. I felt that such a design would lend itself to the use of simpler stitches, all of which you will have seen before in previous projects with the exception of random long-stitch (see Stitch Dictionary, page 14). Some of the shapes have been outlined in cross stitch, and there are detailed inner and outer borders of larger-scale cross stitch.

TIE-BACK

~You Will Need~

For a tie-back measuring 60cm (23½in) across and 16cm (6¼in) deep:

- ❖ 70cm x 43cm (27½in x 17in) 12-gauge canvas
- ❖ Stranded Persian yarn in the colours as given with the chart on pages XIV– XV
- ❖ Tapestry needle
- ❖ 70cm x 43cm (27½in x 17in) firm backing fabric
- ❖ 30cm (12in) twisted cord for loops

STITCHING THE TIE-BACK

Use **two strands only** of Persian yarn throughout, EXCEPT for areas of random long stitch, where you should use **all three strands**. Just over half the chart for the design is shown on pages XIV–XV. Enlarge it to 120% on a photocopier. Trace the full-size design and turn it over to get the mirror-image.

Tape the two sections together to give you the whole tie-back (you only need the centre section once). Trace this onto the canvas, making sure the striped borders follow the vertical canvas threads. Work the design using the stitches and colours given in the keys with the chart.

MAKING UP THE TIE-BACK

Block the tapestry (see page 23) and trim the canvas to 1.5cm (⅝in) all round. Cut the backing fabric to match. With right sides facing, sew the backing fabric to the tapestry, leaving a 25cm (10in) gap at the bottom. Clip the seam allowance, and turn through to the right side. Carefully sew up the opening with slip stitch. Sew a loop of twisted cord of your choice to each end to secure to a hook in the wall.

Work the tie-back using the same colours and stitches as the cushion.

Brilliant shades of gold, green, blue and red make a vivid contrast to the black and white areas of the cushion design.

CUSHION

~You Will Need~

For a cushion measuring 40cm x 41cm (15¼in x 16in):

- 50cm x 51cm (19¼in x 20in) 12-gauge canvas
- Stranded Persian yarn in the colours as given with the chart on pages XVI–XVII
- Tapestry needle
- 44cm x 66cm (17¼in x 26in) piece of firm backing fabric
- 1.8m (2yd) black twisted cord edging
- 40cm x 40cm (16in x 16in) cushion pad

STITCHING THE CUSHION

Use **two strands only** of Persian yarn throughout EXCEPT for areas of random long stitch, where you should use **all three strands.**

Enlarge the chart on pages XVI–XVII to 173% on a photocopier and trace the design onto the canvas, making sure the border lines run along horizontal and vertical canvas threads. Work the outer and inner borders with two rows of red tent stitch separated by two canvas threads. Fill the spaces between the rows with black and yellow cross stitches alternated with red straight stitches. Now work the rest of the design using the stitches and colours given in the keys with the chart.

MAKING UP THE CUSHION

Block the tapestry (see page 23) and trim the excess canvas to leave a 1.5cm (⅝in) seam allowance all round. Cut the backing fabric into two pieces each measuring 44cm x 33cm (17¼in x 13in) and make a 2cm (¾in) hem along one long edge on each piece.

Make up the cushion following the instructions for the Islamic Cushion on page 32.

PLACE MAT & COASTER

The inspiration for this design is the decorative textile work of the Uzbek peoples of Central Asia, who have been making textiles for sale since the mid–nineteenth century. Uzbek bedspreads and hangings are known as suzanis, from the Persian and Tadjik word for 'needle'. Purses, bags, prayer mats, clothing, especially caps — all are densely embroidered with large, isolated floral motifs, and geometric patterns. This project uses many different stitches to add texture. The coaster design is taken from the large central motif on the place mat.

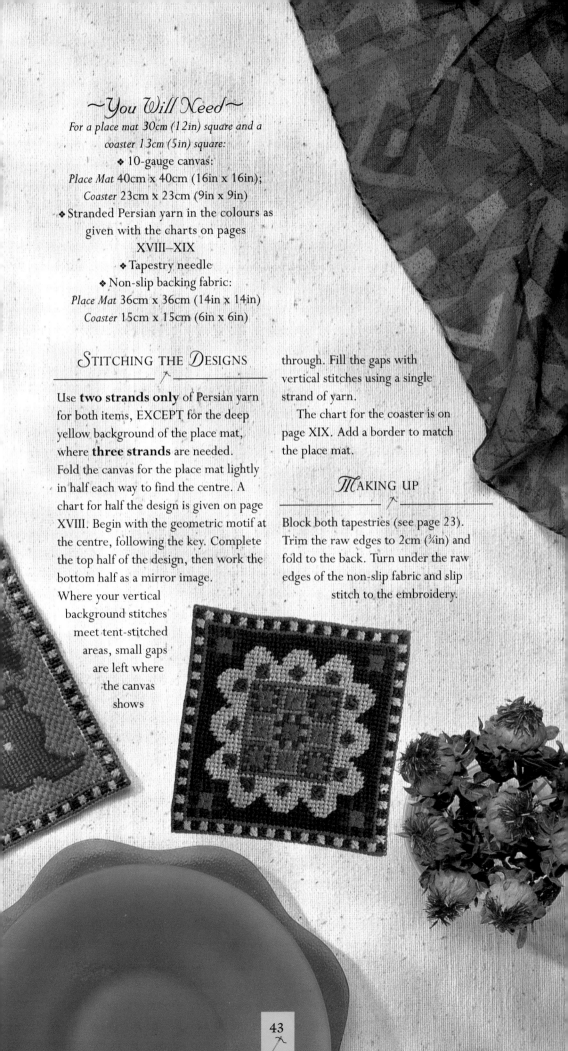

~You Will Need~

For a place mat 30cm (12in) square and a
coaster 13cm (5in) square:
- ❖ 10-gauge canvas:
Place Mat 40cm x 40cm (16in x 16in);
Coaster 23cm x 23cm (9in x 9in)
- ❖ Stranded Persian yarn in the colours as
given with the charts on pages
XVIII–XIX
- ❖ Tapestry needle
- ❖ Non-slip backing fabric:
Place Mat 36cm x 36cm (14in x 14in)
Coaster 15cm x 15cm (6in x 6in)

STITCHING THE DESIGNS

Use **two strands only** of Persian yarn
for both items, EXCEPT for the deep
yellow background of the place mat,
where **three strands** are needed.
Fold the canvas for the place mat lightly
in half each way to find the centre. A
chart for half the design is given on page
XVIII. Begin with the geometric motif at
the centre, following the key. Complete
the top half of the design, then work the
bottom half as a mirror image.
Where your vertical
background stitches
meet tent-stitched
areas, small gaps
are left where
the canvas
shows

through. Fill the gaps with
vertical stitches using a single
strand of yarn.

The chart for the coaster is on
page XIX. Add a border to match
the place mat.

MAKING UP

Block both tapestries (see page 23).
Trim the raw edges to 2cm (¾in) and
fold to the back. Turn under the raw
edges of the non-slip fabric and slip
stitch to the embroidery.

Experiment with blending
yarns to make this
stunning lampshade
covered with fruit of all
kinds. Use the colours
shown here or choose a
range of your own.

FRUIT LAMPSHADE

This design is an introduction to the technique of blending colours. With subtle blending, you can make a smooth transition from the yellow highlight of an apple, for example, through to the deep reds of its shadow, giving a realistic effect. I have concentrated on acidic fruit colours, which give a very bright lampshade. If you wish, you can choose more subdued shades – providing all your colours range from light to dark within each hue, you will achieve the same overall effect.

~You Will Need~

For a lampshade measuring 72cm (28½in) in circumference and 16cm (6¼in) deep:

- ❖ 65cm x 35cm (25½in x 14in) 14-gauge interlock canvas
- ❖ Stranded Persian yarn in the colours as given with the chart on pages XX–XXI
- ❖ Tapestry needle
- ❖ 65cm x 35cm (25½in x 14in) heat-resistant backing fabric
- ❖ Lampshade frame to fit shade

STITCHING

Enlarge the chart on pages XX–XXI to 200% on a photocopier and trace the design squarely onto the canvas. I have used tent stitch throughout this design so that you can concentrate on the blending technique. Use **two strands only** of Persian yarn.

For each fruit, choose the lightest shade and use this to start stitching. As you proceed, you can begin 'dotting' your second shade around the highlight. 'Dotting' is simply breaking up the edge of a stitched area so that there is no hard border between two different shades. Instead, the effect is a soft blend.

If you work your colours outwards in a circular motion, this will help you to form the shapes of most of the fruits (with the obvious exception of the banana). Also, make sure you leave enough room for your shadow colour, as this will give the finished design a strong sense of depth.

The stitching of the leaves is more regimented: they all use the same greens, blending from dark at the base to light at the tip, and the veins are just a single-stitch line of one colour.

When stitching the background, work the darkest shade behind the fruit and blend out into the lighter shade towards the edge of the design.

MAKING UP

Block the tapestry using your template (see page 23). Trim the excess canvas and join the two straight edges with right sides together, using backstitch. Sew to the frame. Line the shade with lining paper or fabric (check with the retailer that your chosen lining material is sufficiently heat-resistant). Trim the top and bottom of the lampshade with cord or braid of your choice.

Twelve Houses Cushion

Inspired by architectural styles, this cushion cover is made up of twelve different house fronts. There are various tapestry stitches that lend themselves to the forming of brickwork patterns, and against these I have picked out the windows and doors in finer tent or cross stitch. The more textured stitches of the foliage provide a contrast to the predominantly geometric design.

This project is ideal for using up leftover lengths of yarn. Any spare thread can be used to pick out the details of windows, curtains and climbing plants, as long as it is bright enough to stand out from the background colours.

~You Will Need~

For a cushion measuring 53cm (21in) square:

❖ 63 x 63cm (26in x 26in) 10-gauge double canvas
❖ Stranded Persian yarn in the colours as given with the chart on pages XXII–XXIV
❖ Tapestry needle
❖ Two 56cm x 34cm (22in x 13½in) pieces backing fabric
❖ 2.5m (3yd) black piping
❖ Cushion pad to fit

Stitching

Use **two strands only** of Persian yarn throughout. Enlarge the chart on pages XXII–XXIV to 180% on a photocopier. You will need to enlarge it in sections onto several sheets of paper and then tape these together to achieve the full-size pattern. You can now trace the design onto the canvas, making sure that the border lines run along horizontal and vertical canvas threads so that the houses are positioned squarely.

The chart and keys show the various stitches and yarn colours needed to complete each of the patchwork houses. Begin stitching the houses at the centre of the canvas and work gradually outwards.

When all the houses are complete, add a cream border in cushion stitch edged with rows of black tent stitch. Each cushion stitch is worked over five canvas threads each way.

Making Up

Block the canvas (see page 23). Trim the excess canvas to leave 1.5cm (⅝in) all round. Make up the cushion in the same way as given for the Islamic Cushion on page 32.

CONCLUSION

*O*nce you have tried some of the projects in this book, you will begin to develop a feeling for working with wool and canvas, and you will hopefully feel inspired to dream up some designs of your own. To give your creativity a boost, indulge yourself with a selection of yarns in beautiful colours and experiment with different combinations of the stitches shown in the Stitch Dictionary on pages 14–19.

Tapestry is a craft that can rapidly become a passion and you may well find that you are never without a piece of work on the go. Luckily, a rolled-up canvas and some yarn are easily portable, so you can take your tapestry with you on journeys or on holiday and do a little stitching whenever you have a spare moment.

CONVERSION CHART

If you are unable to obtain Paterna Persian yarn as specified for the projects, you can substitute the shades of DMC or Anchor tapestry wool listed here. The shades given are the best equivalent to the Paterna range, but they may not be absolutely exact.

Paterna	DMC	Anchor	Paterna	DMC	Anchor	Paterna	DMC	Anchor
220	7309	9800	662	7541	9006	841	7606	8200
221	7624	9768	670	7583	9198	842	7850	8214
263	ecru	8002	671	7584	9274	843	7851	8212
300	7708	8528	672	7681	9282	851	7920	8238
303	7896	8524	673	7470	9192	852	7125	8234
310	7259	8530	680	7943	8990	853	7873	8232
324	7251	8522	682	7911	8988	860	7920	8236
340	7796	8610	685	7912	8986	862	7356	8162
342	7798	8608	690	7427	9180	870	7169	8264
421	7489	9648	691	7367	9206	880	7446	8312
462	7413	9366	692	7769	9156	900	7219	8426
480	7449	9602	693	7548	9196	902	7138	8424
D516	7428	8992	700	7767	8140	903	7602	8420
530	7429	8906	702	7472	8098	904	7603	8416
540	7820	8694	710	7784	8120	905	7804	8452
541	7318	8692	711	7785	8098	910	7212	8426
542	7317	8690	712	7726	8018	912	7205	8418
544	7314	8688	714	7905	8052	925	7211	8412
551	7317	8674	720	7446	9538	930	7758	8402
580	7311	8824	722	7445	9526	931	7196	8400
581	7650	8822	724	7783	8140	940	7137	8442
610	7385	9008	760	7431	8094	941	7640	8216
611	7320	9022	763	7351	8112	942	7136	8440
612	7384	9100	770	7436	8124	950	7544	8218
645	7727	9322	801	7437	8156	953	7104	8436
653	7361	9306	820	7606	8198	964	7211	8482
660	7389	9028	830	7360	8238	970	7666	8202
661	7540	8992	840	7108	8204			

CANVAS, YARN AND NEEDLE CHART

This chart shows the number of strands of yarn you will need to achieve the best coverage of each gauge of canvas. The yarns included are crewel wool, Persian yarn and tapestry wool. The most suitable needle sizes are shown.

CANVAS GAUGE	YARN (number of strands per type)	NEEDLE SIZE
14 or 12 gauge	3 crewel 2 or 3 Persian 1 tapestry	20
10 gauge	3 or 4 crewel 2 or 3 Persian 1 tapestry 1 tapestry with 1 crewel	20 or 18
8 gauge	1 tapestry with 1 crewel 3 or 4 Persian	18 or 16

I

ROSE SQUARE

KEY

1 skein in each of:

- □ white 263
- ■ black 530
- + blue 580
- / light pink 905
- × middle pink 904
- ✗ dark pink 900
- ▽ light green 612
- ▼ dark green 680

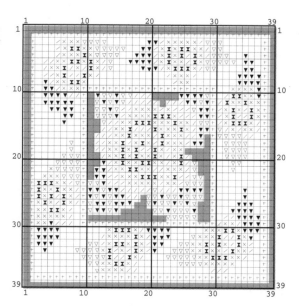

PRIMULA SQUARE

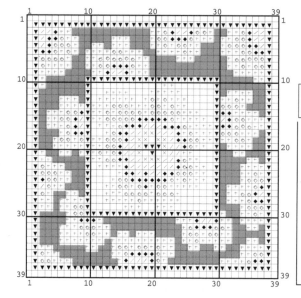

KEY

1 skein in each of:

- + light blue 544
- ◇ mid blue 542
- ◆ dark blue 541
- / cream 263
- × yellow 763
- □ light green 693
- ▼ dark green 691
- ■ orange 700

DAISY SQUARE

KEY

1 skein in each of:

- + light green 685
- ◇ mid green 682
- ◆ dark green 611
- □ yellow 702
- × dark yellow 700
- ▷ orange 851
- ▶ red 840
- ■ black 530

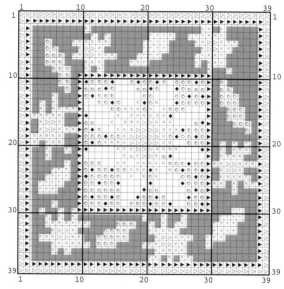

FARMYARD PANEL

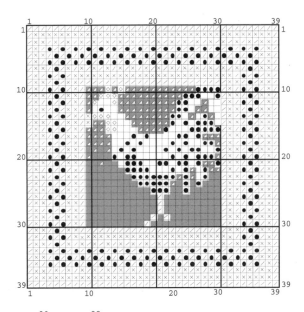

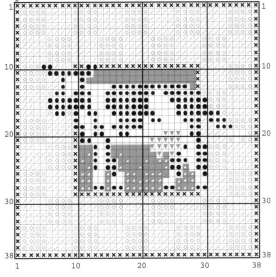

KEY

1 skein in each of:

/	yellow 711
✕	brown 480
●	black 220
■	light green 612
◨	dark green 610
◇	red 841
□	white 263
▼	dark pink 912
✕	orange 862
▽	light pink 925

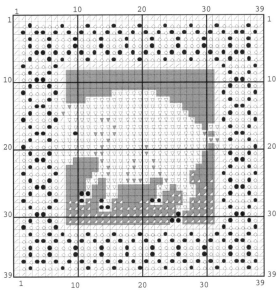

Floral Cushion

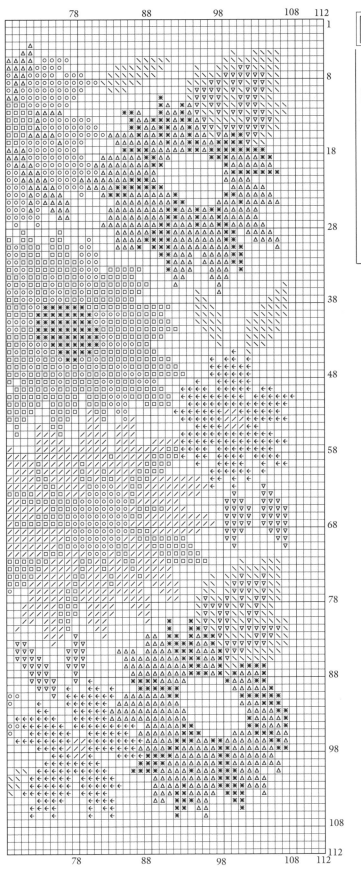

KEY

Number of skeins
in brackets ( ):

/   cream 645 (3)

▫   yellow 702 (3)

○   orange 853 (3)

△   red 950 (3)

✳   brown 480 (2)

←   blue 551 (3)

\   green 693 (2)

▽   dark green 691 (2)

▫   black 531 –
       background (10)

FISH PICTURE

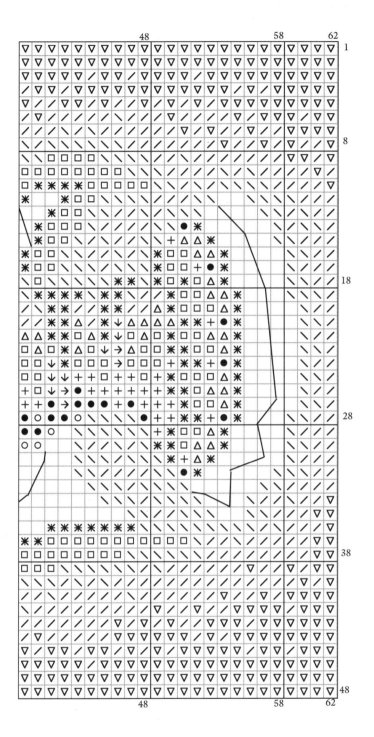

- ❖ Work in tent stitch unless stitching the areas detailed below.
- ❖ French knots are denoted by light grey circles. Work them following the written instructions on page 31.
- ❖ The gills and fins are worked in satin stitch. The solid black lines on the chart indicate the blending of colours. You may find it helpful to use the picture and instructions on pages 30 – 31 as a guide when you are working these areas of the design.

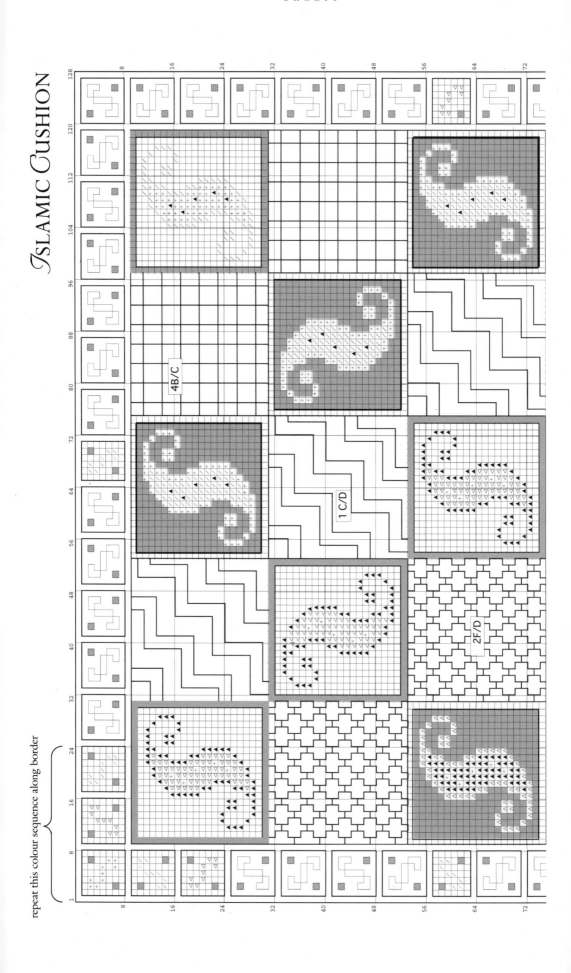

ISLAMIC CUSHION

4B/C

1 C/D

2F/D

repeat this colour sequence along border

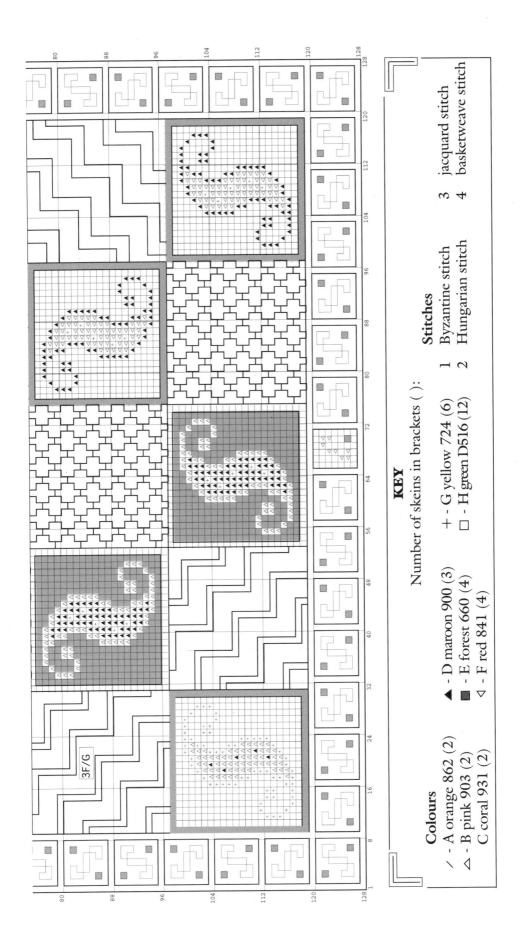

3F/G

KEY

Number of skeins in brackets ( ):

Colours

╱ - A orange 862 (2)	▲ - D maroon 900 (3)	+ - G yellow 724 (6)
△ - B pink 903 (2)	■ - E forest 660 (4)	□ - H green D516 (12)
C coral 931 (2)	▽ - F red 841 (4)	

Stitches

| 1 | Byzantine stitch | 3 | jacquard stitch |
| 2 | Hungarian stitch | 4 | basketweave stitch |

NOËL, NOËL

BAUBLE

KEY
1 skein in each of:
▼ dark red 840
╱ yellow 710
□ purple 300
◇ metallic gold

BELL

KEY
1 skein in each of:
▼ green 682
□ crimson 941
◇ metallic gold

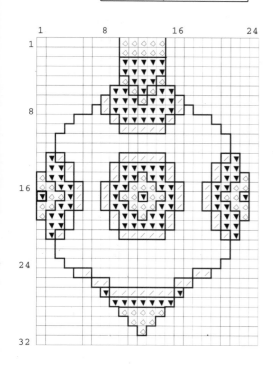

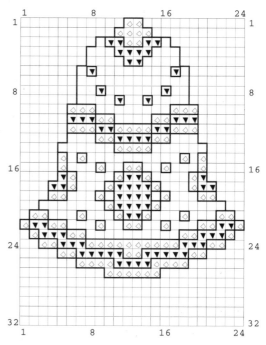

ROBIN

KEY
1 skein in each of:
▼ black 220
▽ white 263
○ scarlet 820
□ brown 870
╱ metallic gold

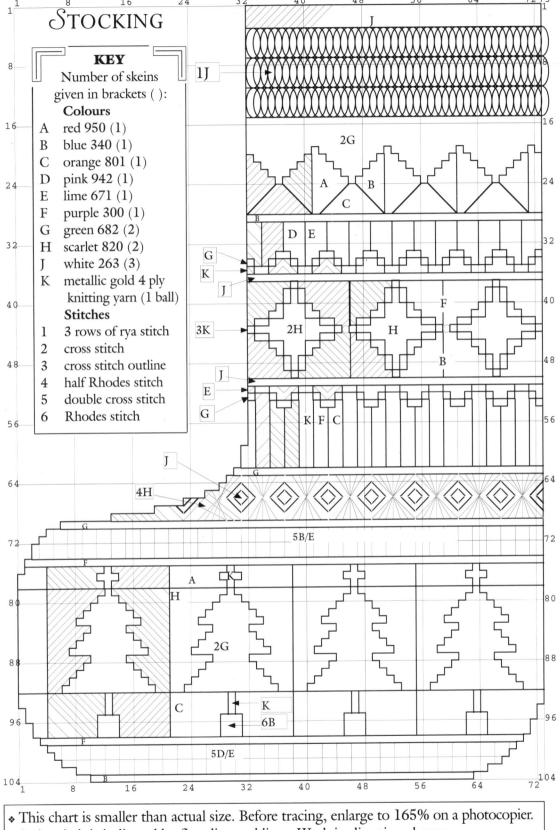

STOCKING

KEY
Number of skeins
given in brackets ( ):
Colours
A red 950 (1)
B blue 340 (1)
C orange 801 (1)
D pink 942 (1)
E lime 671 (1)
F purple 300 (1)
G green 682 (2)
H scarlet 820 (2)
J white 263 (3)
K metallic gold 4 ply
knitting yarn (1 ball)
Stitches
1 3 rows of rya stitch
2 cross stitch
3 cross stitch outline
4 half Rhodes stitch
5 double cross stitch
6 Rhodes stitch

♦ This chart is smaller than actual size. Before tracing, enlarge to 165% on a photocopier.
♦ Satin stitch is indicated by fine diagonal lines. Work in direction shown.
♦ All single horizontal rows are in tent stitch.
♦ All green zigzag single rows are in cross stitch.
♦ Gold stars and tree trunks are in cross stitch.

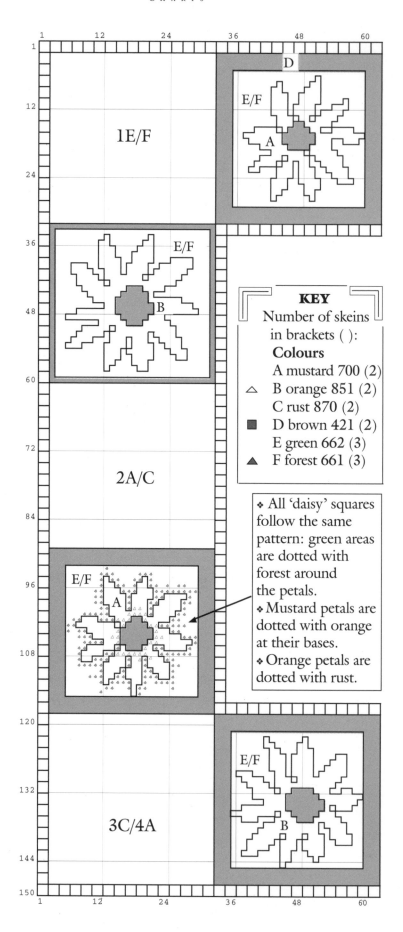

KEY

Number of skeins in brackets ( ):

Colours

A mustard 700 (2)
△ B orange 851 (2)
C rust 870 (2)
■ D brown 421 (2)
E green 662 (3)
▲ F forest 661 (3)

❖ All 'daisy' squares follow the same pattern: green areas are dotted with forest around the petals.
❖ Mustard petals are dotted with orange at their bases.
❖ Orange petals are dotted with rust.

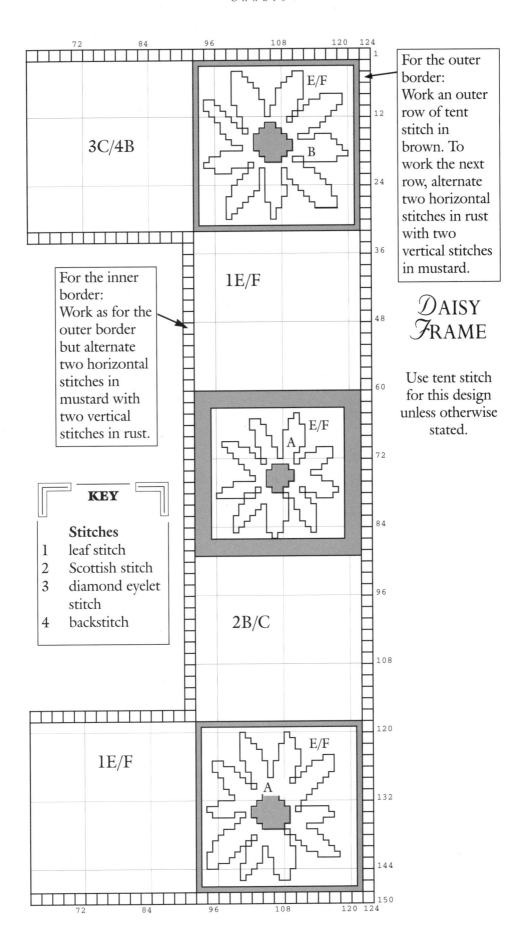

For the outer border: Work an outer row of tent stitch in brown. To work the next row, alternate two horizontal stitches in rust with two vertical stitches in mustard.

3C/4B

E/F

B

1E/F

For the inner border: Work as for the outer border but alternate two horizontal stitches in mustard with two vertical stitches in rust.

*D*AISY *F*RAME

Use tent stitch for this design unless otherwise stated.

E/F

A

KEY

Stitches
1 leaf stitch
2 Scottish stitch
3 diamond eyelet stitch
4 backstitch

2B/C

1E/F

E/F

A

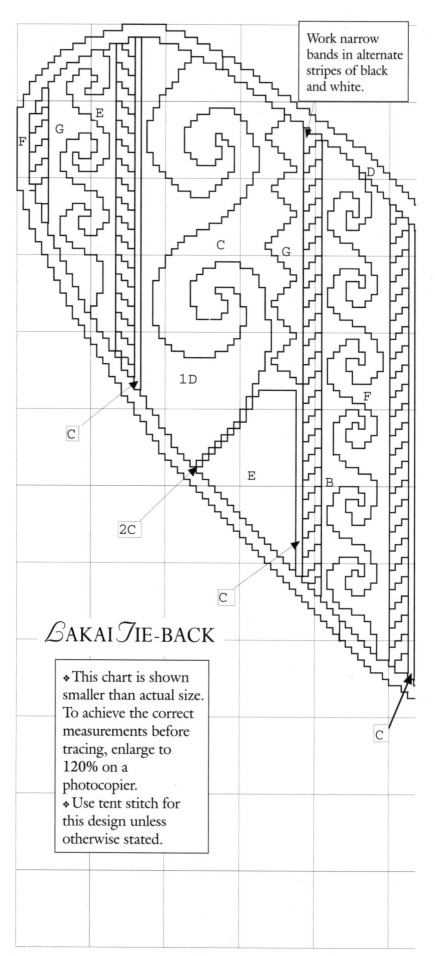

Work narrow bands in alternate stripes of black and white.

E

G

F

D

C

G

1D

C

2C

F

C

E

B

$\mathcal{L}$AKAI $\mathcal{T}$IE-BACK

❖ This chart is shown smaller than actual size. To achieve the correct measurements before tracing, enlarge to 120% on a photocopier.
❖ Use tent stitch for this design unless otherwise stated.

C

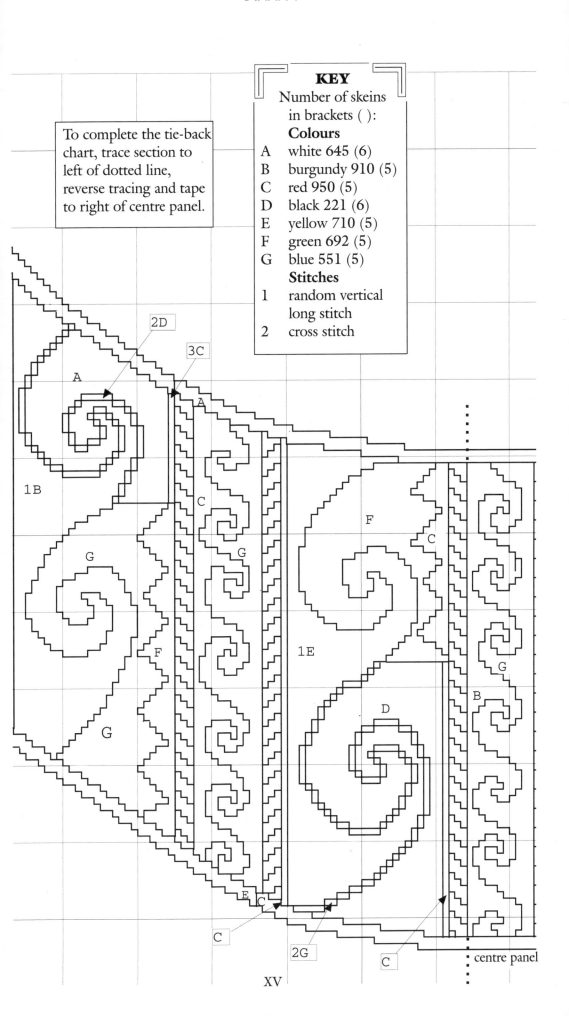

To complete the tie-back
chart, trace section to
left of dotted line,
reverse tracing and tape
to right of centre panel.

KEY
Number of skeins
in brackets ( ):
Colours
A   white 645 (6)
B   burgundy 910 (5)
C   red 950 (5)
D   black 221 (6)
E   yellow 710 (5)
F   green 692 (5)
G   blue 551 (5)
Stitches
1   random vertical
    long stitch
2   cross stitch

2D

3C

A

A

1B

C

G

G

F

C

F

C

G

G

1E

D

B

G

E C

C

2G

C

centre panel

ℒakai Cushion

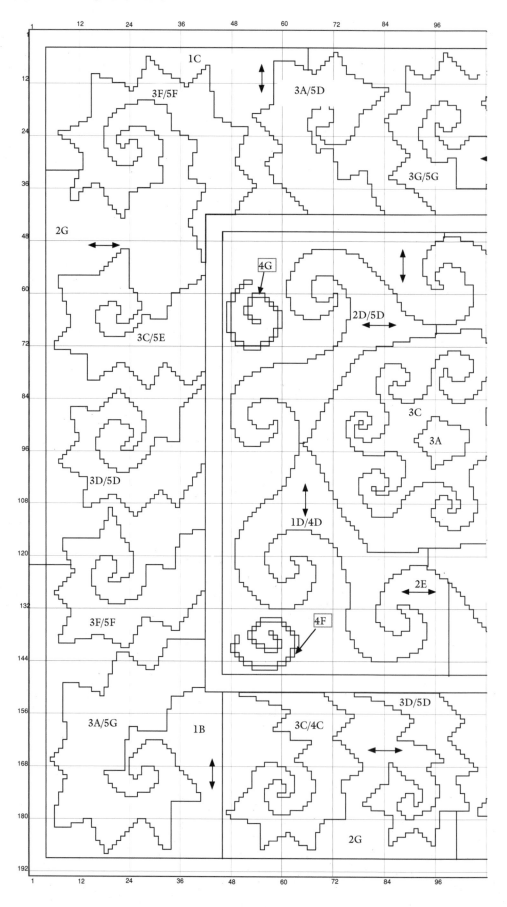

last stitch 193

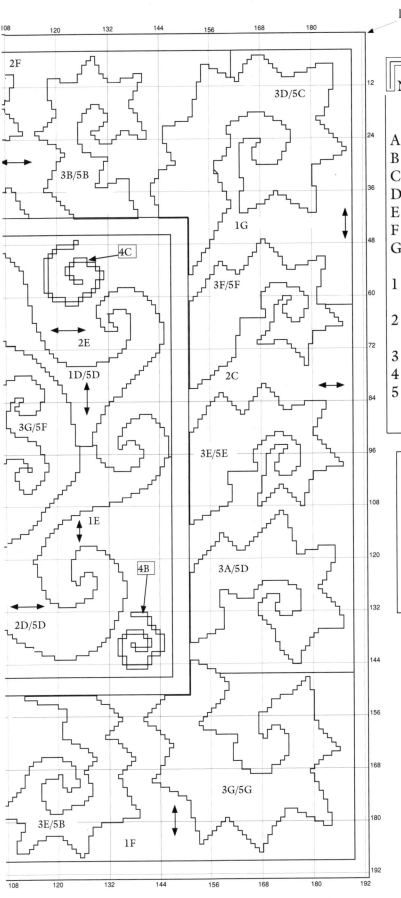

KEY
Number of skeins in brackets ( ):

Colours

A   white 645 (3)
B   burgundy 910 (3)
C   red 950 (6)
D   black 221 (7)
E   yellow 710 (8)
F   green 692 (8)
G   blue 551 (8)

Stitches

1   random vertical
    long stitch
2   random horizontal
    long stitch
3   tent stitch
4   cross stitch
5   outline in
    cross stitch

❖ This chart is
shown smaller than
actual size. To
achieve the correct
measurements
before tracing,
enlarge to 173%
on a photocopier.

XVII

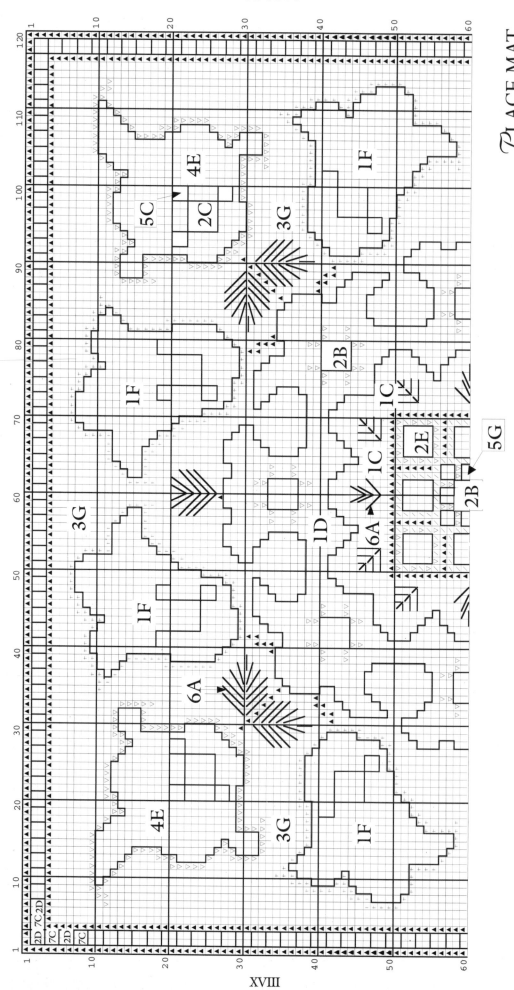

PLACE MAT

XVIII

COASTER

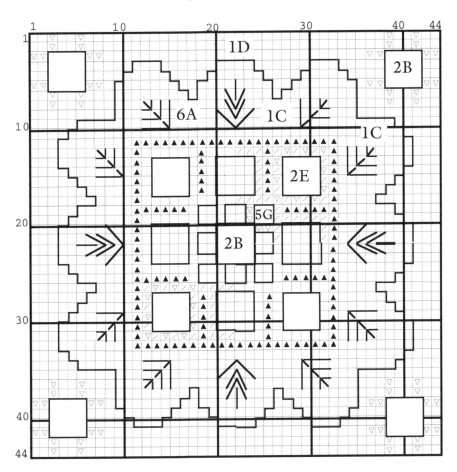

❖ Work these designs by counting the squares on the charts rather than by tracing the designs onto the canvas.

KEY

Number of skeins in brackets ( ):

Placemat	Coaster		Stitches
A forest 661 (1)	A forest 661 (1)	1	tent stitch
▲ B blue 581 (2)	▲ B blue 581 (1)	2	Algerian eye stitch
C green 653 (4)	C green 653 (1)	3	brick stitch
D brown 421 (5)	D brown 421 (1)	4	cross stitch
+ E orange 852 (5)	+ E orange 852 (1)	5	double cross stitch
▽ F red 840 (5)	▽ F red 840 (1)	6	leaf stitch
╱ G gold 700 (7)	╱ G gold 700 (1)	7	mosaic stitch

For leaves: Leaf stitch variations – work in forest in the direction shown.
For border: Alternate 2 x 2 squares of Algerian eye stitch in brown and mosaic stitch in green.
Symbolled squares: Use cross stitch in the correct colours for ▽ and + and tent stitch for ▲ and ╱.

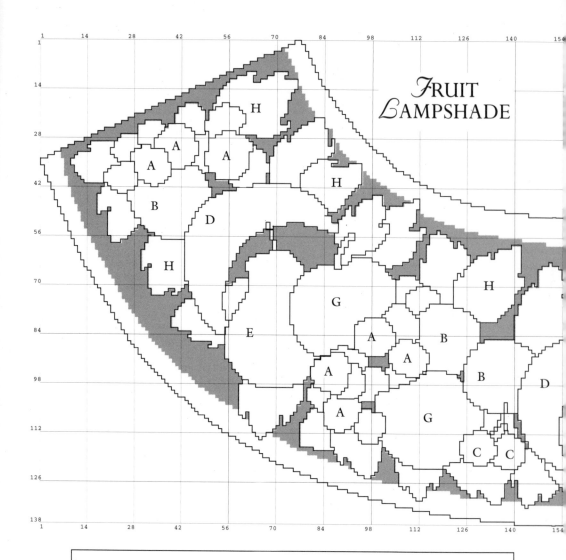

FRUIT LAMPSHADE

❖ This chart is shown smaller than actual size. To achieve the correct measurements before tracing, enlarge to 200% on a photocopier.

KEY

Start with one skein of each of the following colours, adding to them if necessary as they run out:

Violets	300	Greens	530	Yellows	700	Reds	840
	303		612		710		841
	324		670		712		842
			671		714		843
Blues	320		672		720		904
	340		673		760		940
	342		680		763		953
	540		682		801		964
			690				970
			693				

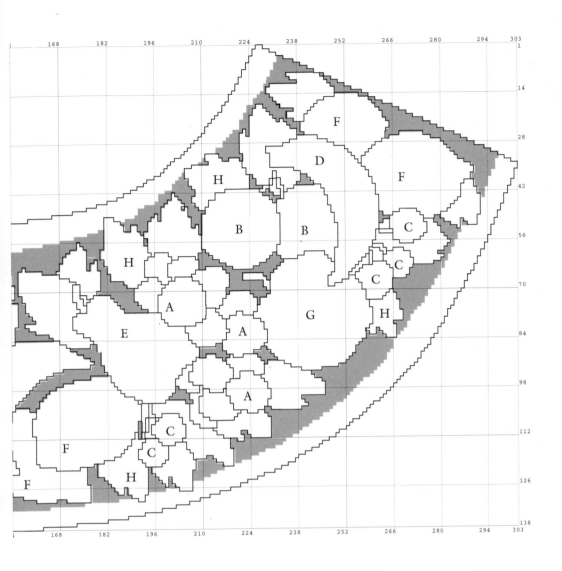

COLOUR GUIDE FOR WORKING THE LAMPSHADE

(Note that some colours are used for more than one area of the design)

Grapes A	540		712		843
	340		714		693
	342				670
		Pears E	710		801
Plums B	320		801		714
	300		842		
	303		720	**Leaves H**	693
	324		840		612
	904				690
		Lemons F	760		670
Cherries C	940		763		673
	953		672		
	970		671	**Background (shaded)**	
	964		670		530
					682
Bananas D	700	**Apples G**	970		680
	710		841		

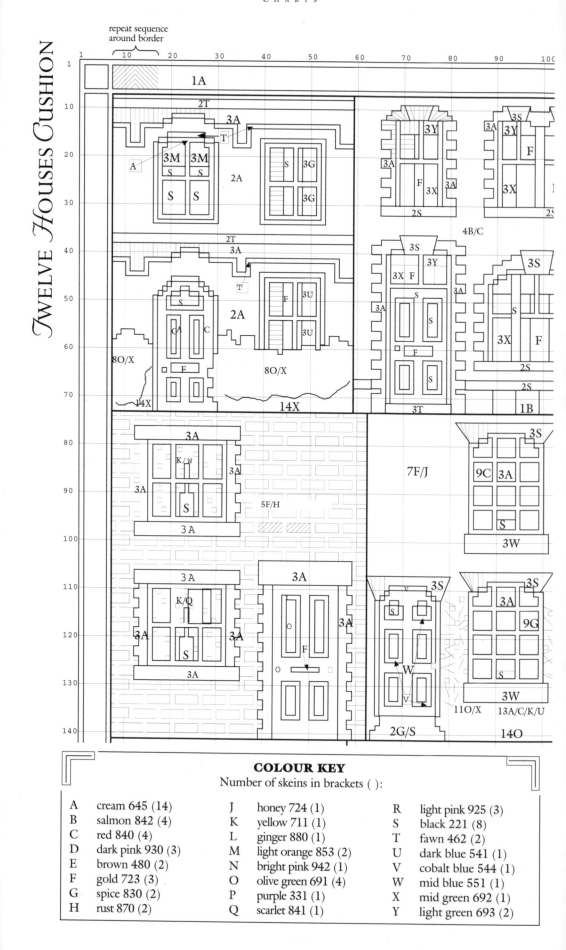

TWELVE HOUSES CUSHION

repeat sequence around border

COLOUR KEY
Number of skeins in brackets ( ):

A	cream 645 (14)	J	honey 724 (1)	R	light pink 925 (3)
B	salmon 842 (4)	K	yellow 711 (1)	S	black 221 (8)
C	red 840 (4)	L	ginger 880 (1)	T	fawn 462 (2)
D	dark pink 930 (3)	M	light orange 853 (2)	U	dark blue 541 (1)
E	brown 480 (2)	N	bright pink 942 (1)	V	cobalt blue 544 (1)
F	gold 723 (3)	O	olive green 691 (4)	W	mid blue 551 (1)
G	spice 830 (2)	P	purple 331 (1)	X	mid green 692 (1)
H	rust 870 (2)	Q	scarlet 841 (1)	Y	light green 693 (2)

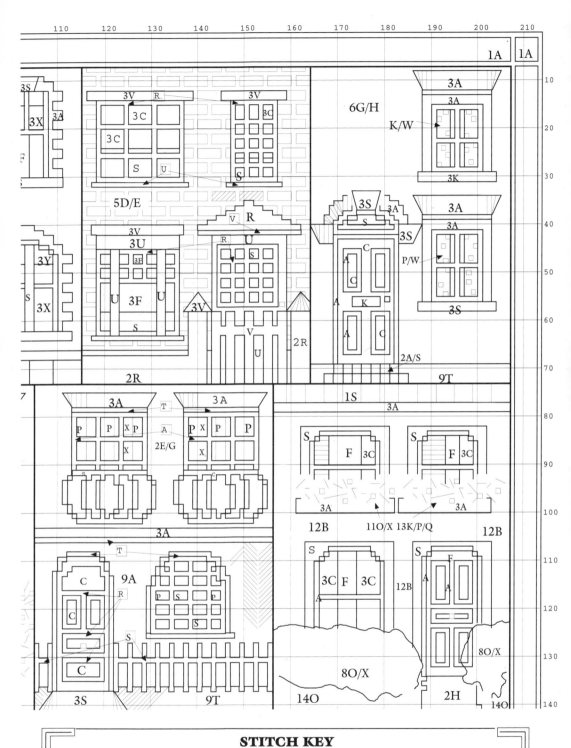

STITCH KEY

1	cushion stitch	9	diagonal satin stitch
2	mosaic stitch	10	horizontal Algerian filling stitch
3	satin stitch	11	random satin stitch
4	double cross stitch	12	brick stitch
5	Scottish stitch	13	French knots
6	horizontal Hungarian stitch	14	cross stitch
7	vertical Hungarian stitch		
8	velvet stitch		

bottom left-hand side

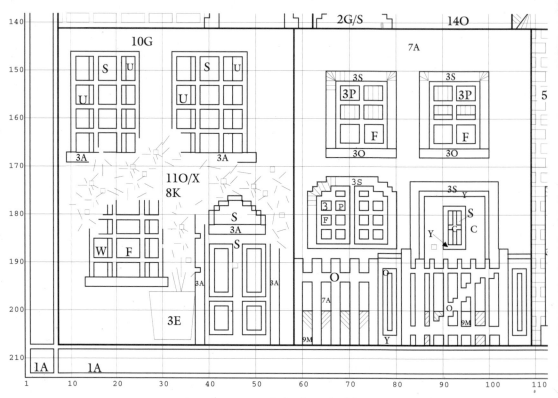

bottom right-hand side

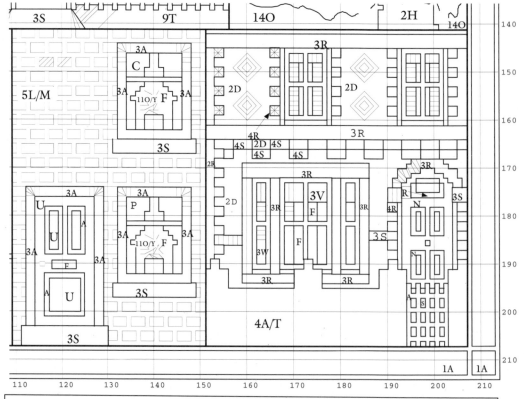

❖ Work the diagonal stitches in the Scottish stitch house fronts over 2 x 5 holes for the long bricks and over 2 x 3 holes for the short bricks.

❖ Where a stitch is not specified, use tent stitch

❖ Enlarge chart to 200% on a photocopier, then trace.